29 DEADLY SIGILS

TO HARM, GAIN CONTROL OR DISARM

SIGILS DEVELOPED WITH

THE BOY

... A DAEMON FROM THE HOCKOMOCK SWAMP

BY

SORCERESS CAGLIASTRO

PUBLISHED BY IRON RING PUBLISHING

DEDICATION

To the one who never leaves….
We have protected one another for so long…this is only the beginning of our road….meat is best served hot and rare…

WARNING
DO NOT SHARE THIS BOOK.
PLACE YOUR BLOOD IN THIS CIRCLE.

THIS IS BLOOD SORCERY........

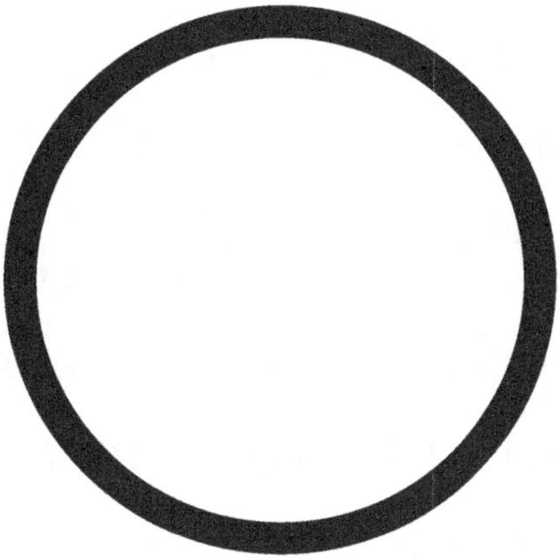

NOTE - YOU WILL BE ASKED TO COPY THE SIGILS, READ THOSE INSTRUCTIONS CAREFULLY...

TABLE OF CONTENTS

(TOC CONTINUED)

PERSONAL FORWARD

When I feel anger - my saliva immediately tastes like Blood.

That is part of the skillset of a Blood Sorceress and Necromancer.... My Attending Daemons, 1 through 9, and 4 others save my life every day as they, and most especially 9, and a few Disincarnate that are always by my side... they help me through the exhaustive process of navigating the other less familiar Disincarnate and the Daemons that are in my life, seeking attention and communication all day, every day...

That being said I am also so very grateful for the students and the associates who dare to spend their lives in this work….without them and their vigilance I would go into the woods – perhaps even the **Urban** woods, and write alone with my inhabitants….ah the glamour…

This book troubles me because its contents are so powerful - and now here I have made it available for you, the reader to either destroy your enemies – or prop up your air conditioners with it – that is, of course, up to you…

The question, I suppose, is not what you do with it per se – the question is what you **CAN** do with it – and that is all on you, the reader/practitioner once you begin…

Everyone who comes to this work wants to be a wizard and summon armies of the dead, shoot lightning bolts from their fingers, encounter dragons and ancient warlords, find the perfect lover, grow a huge phallus, produce a child where a womb has repeatedly failed, they want to cure cancer and have great minds, own a half million dollar sports car, have their acne disappear, no longer be allergic to shellfish, kill off their ex-spouse, make themselves and their children well and wake up in a world perfect for them.....

That's the funny thing about the Science of Sorcery, get it just right and all of that is possible...

There are many paths, I know because I too have tried them and like so many others have left them...

However this is the Science of Sorcery and like all good scientists we gather and review data, and the data has produced a result that is of no surprise whatsoever to me.... Nearly all of those who take this ride with me – through the Science of Sorcery, the sigil work, the "4Pillars + the 5th Pillar", the working with Disincarnate and Daemons and all of the associated aspects of this process....they stay – right here – in this lane – on this path – because it delivers....

See closing comments for more specific venom.......

Giddy Up..........

SORCERESS CAGLIASTRO,
Blood Sorceress, Necromancer in the hands of 9

HISTORY, HOW THESE SIGILS CAME TO BE.....

I am not one to buy into the hype of "haunted places" – or generally "inhabited places" – as I live in the constant presence of the Disincarnate and the "haunted places" way of thinking is usually some "ghost hunter" nonsense…they are everywhere – they look over your shoulder as you read this…. That being said I must share the story of the Forest. I live in the center of the Bridgewater Triangle in Southern Massachusetts. Dighton is the only town in the triangle that is **completely** inside of it – as all the other towns leak outside of its borders. North Dighton is particularly bound in – by its forests, its Daemons, and its odd landlords who tend to own property here - yet live elsewhere.

It is the phenomenon of cowards to gain from the courageous living of others....

What was gained here originated in **my** forest – which, allow me to be clear – I do not own on paper. This Forest and the Tiny House came to me as the product of Sorcery – I received exactly what I conceived through Sorcery....

This Forest does not care a bit about who's signature holds ownership – it cares only that once I arrived, and accepted the Daemons therein – it flourished and like a lover's heart - it will – even once I leave - never see itself as "belonging" to anyone else....
How does this concern the sigils...?

One **must**, in order to utilize these sigils, create an effigy of the co-maker. THE BOY who came from the Hockomonk Swamp to my door to assist me in the destruction of all that must be destroyed.

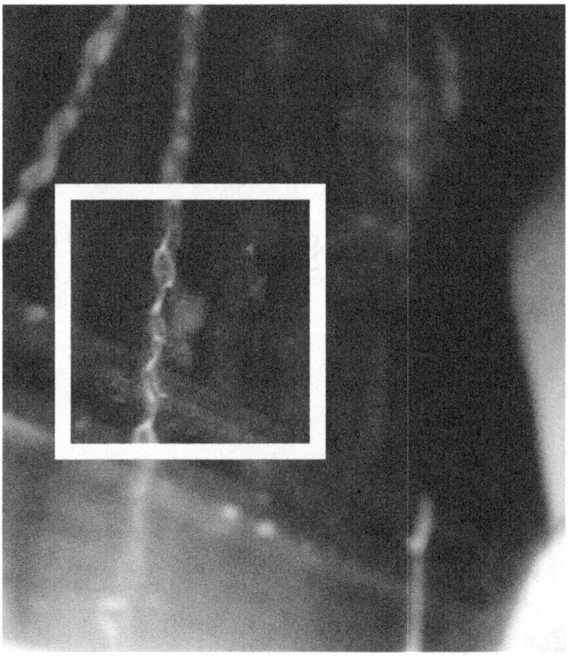

For now read on – instructions for the effigy will follow in the next section....

THE BOY has developed a particular hatred for the woman who owns the property on which I live, and that hatred becomes more and more apparent as he has a general distaste for anyone who states papered ownership of the forests and swamp lands of this small area. I personally could care less about her…he is a Daemon and will do with her as he pleases – I have other things to do - such as write this book….

I digress….

Back to the subject at hand – which is how best to use the sigils in this book. First I must say that they exist through my relationship with THE BOY, and the images he has provided in the wet earth that sits along the muddied edges of the foul swamp.

I sit, for hours, at the edge of the swamp, and see with the efforts of Divination all those who have died there either by choice, accident or against their will....

Who then is THE BOY?

There was a woman there at the edges of the Hockomock Swamp, her year feels like 1749...the woman who lived alongside - and stepped into the swamp many times, living nearby off the land. People came and went and took their way with her and she bore many children.
THE BOY tells me that sixteen and one half (?) children were born to her... They were products of her anguish and she treated them poorly. Many died – others were put to death – and she eventually joined them. All of their bodies rotted into the swamp....

THE BOY is a Daemon…

Daemons however are an amalgam, a collection of sorrow and anguish and they lack the understanding humans have, that Daemons form, and may – should they be strong or even just clear in their thinking, develop so that they become mobile – some can just up and go. They can leave.

Despite my consistent discussion of this matter, many humans with an interest in Daemons either do not know this, or have made the decision to continue on in the misconfiguration of the connection from Daemons to doctrines…..

So the woman suffered with the living children, suffered to care for them, suffered to love them though she in fact did not – suffered against hating them which is a battle she most often lost, and most of all – suffered enough to fight against occasionally bludgeoning them and tossing them into the swamp.

On occasion – on many occasions she lost that battle. THE BOY was never a living human, nor a dead one. He is a product of the sorrow – an effect of hatred and longing and sadness, of lacking and losing and begging for death – from this he arose. He came from the cumulus, the gathering of dismay and in that he formed his own container, THE BOY, not an imitation – rather a walking existence of giggling revenge…and now he is in my court….

What of the swamp? What is **thought** is often anathema to what is **known,** and in rare cases the combination of the two are worse than that which could be imagined...

For periods throughout the 1600's, the Hockomock Swamp was used as a fortress by the Wampanoag which were the predominate tribe in the area. They used this vast wetlands in this way to protect them against invasion by early white settlers.
Metacomet (also known as King Philip) used it as a strategic base of operations during what came to be known as King Philip's War. From the Hockomonk Swamp, defensive and offensive assaults were launched upon nearby white settlements.

During the 1700s and 1800s, white settlers deemed the swamp to be worthless barren land and attempted to drain it and convert it into profitable farmland. This was of course met with great distain from the indigenous people who knew the real importance of the swamp. Benjamin Drake of Easton and later William L. Chaffin were early advocates of the plan to drain the swamp. The indigenous people of the region placed a higher value on the swamp. For centuries, they had relied on it for a great hunting ground, and due to its ability to provide game and therefore sustenance, the swamp had gained a revered status among them. They named it Hockomock meaning "place where spirits dwell".

There are many stories and legends that have become associated with the area and the swamp, however I will not, in this writing or otherwise, support the makers of these legends as they are paranormal "ghost hunters" and people who lead tourists to stomp on the graves of others in very old local cemeteries so that they have a reason to play dress up and garner a few coins. Allow me share my personal experience...

When I arrived here and I made an effort to attend a "table tipping event" at a local "antique" shop in Bridgewater. I reserved a space on the site for myself and my daughter.

A hideous sea hag of a woman called to inform me that the other two sea hags who own the shop and their fake white light nonsense "medium" forbade me to attend. Ms. K it seemed, did not want me in the room as she tipped her table…

I am sure the reader can see that she did not desire to be called upon as a horrid fake pulling on the heart strings of those in mourning….

From this same location come the troops of cos-play grave stompers who feed their filthy mouths from the coins they receive when guiding tourists to dig their heels into quiet graves, and try to catch glimpses of the Disincarnate who are trapped in their own loop in that poor invaded cemetery.

None of them, of course, leave a drop of Blood or offer a ritual of respect....we are talking about the abusers of the dead....

From this culture, the same culture that tore down the indigenous people, these New Englanders who dress up and stomp on the graves of their own ancestors came the woman who produced the children whose sorrow produced THE BOY.
He will feed on them for as long as he sees fit, and I will help him do so by sharing his sigils, his image and his story with whomever chooses to listen...

BLANK PAGE FOR NOTES

29 DEADLY SIGILS TO HARM, GAIN CONTROL OR DISARM

1. TO ALLOW YOURSELF TO DO DAMAGING WORKS

2. GO AHEAD....JUMP

3. TO CAUSE SOMEONE TO LIE ALL THE TIME AGAINST THEIR WILL

4. TO STOP ANOTHER FROM FEELING JOY

5. TO CAUSE SOMEONE TO FOREVER DESIRE WHAT THEY CANNOT HAVE

6. TO TAKE AWAY SOMEONE'S ABILITY TO ORGASM

7. TO CAUSE ONE TO CONFESS TO A CRIME THEY DID NOT COMMIT

8. TO KEEP ONE STUCK IN SORROW

9. TO INJECT ONESELF INTO SEXUAL DREAMS

10. TO STEAL AWAY THE LOVE OF AN "INFANT"

11. TO SHUT SOMEONE'S MOUTH COMPLETELY

12. TO CAUSE DESTRUCTION THROUGH SUGGESTION OF POSSESSION

13. TO FORCE DISTANCE BETWEEN TWO HUMANS

14. TO CAUSE SOMEONE TO FORGET THEIR IDENTITY

15. TO CAUSE ONE TO SELF-DESTRUCT THROUGH GUILT

16. TO ENCOURAGE SELF-LOATHING

17. TO CAUSE SOMEONE TO THINK THEY ARE SOMEONE ELSE OF YOUR CHOICE

18. TO MAKE SOMEONE PAY, WITH THEIR WELLNESS OR LONGEVITY, FOR WASTING YOUR TIME OR TRUST (THE BROTHER SIGIL TO THE POISONER'S SIGIL)

19. TO HAVE YOUR WORDS HEARD AS DEADLY

20. TO INCREASE UN-WELLNESS IN INCREMENTS

21. TO ALLOW FOR PROFOUND AND OBVIOUS HUMILIATING DECLINING OF ANOTHER

22. TO CAUSE ONE TO BE TRAPPED IN A LOOP

23. TO FORCE SOMEONE TO LIVE IN THE PAST

24. TO MAKE SOMEONE VULNERABLE TO POSSESSION

25. TO CAUSE ONE TO HEAR CONSTANT NOISE

26. TO CAUSE A COMA THAT MIMICS DEATH

27. TO CAUSE A LANDLORD TO BE DESTROYED

28. TO CAUSE A LIAR'S TONGUE TO SWELL AND CHOKE THEM

29. TO INVITE THE ACTION OF DEATH INTO SOMEONE'S HOME

BLANK PAGE FOR NOTES

29DS-I TO ALLOW YOURSELF TO DO DAMAGING WORKS

29DS-II GO
AHEAD....JUMP

29DS-III TO CAUSE SOMEONE TO LIE ALL THE TIME AGAINST THEIR WILL

29DS-IV TO STOP ANOTHER FROM FEELING JOY

29DS-V TO CAUSE SOMEONE TO FOREVER DESIRE WHAT THEY CANNOT HAVE

29DS-VI TO TAKE AWAY SOMEONE'S ABILITY TO ORGASM

29DS-VII TO CAUSE ONE TO CONFESS TO A CRIME THEY DID NOT COMMIT

29DS-VIII TO KEEP ONE STUCK IN SORROW

29DS-IX TO INJECT ONESELF INTO SEXUAL DREAMS

29DS-X TO STEAL AWAY THE LOVE OF AN "INFANT"

29DS-XI TO SHUT SOMEONE'S MOUTH COMPLETELY

29DS-XII TO CAUSE DESTRUCTION THROUGH SUGGESTION OF POSSESSION

29DS-XIII
TO FORCE DISTANCE BETWEEN TWO HUMANS

29DS-XIV TO CAUSE SOMEONE TO FORGET THEIR IDENTITY

29DS-XV
TO CAUSE ONE TO SELF-DESTRUCT THROUGH GUILT

29DS-XVI
TO ENCOURAGE SELF-LOATHING

29DS-XVII TO CAUSE SOMEONE TO THINK THEY ARE SOMEONE ELSE OF YOUR CHOICE

29DS-XVIII TO MAKE SOMEONE PAY, WITH THEIR WELLNESS OR LONGEVITY, FOR WASTING YOUR TIME OR TRUST

(THE BROTHER SIGIL TO THE POISONER'S SIGIL)

29DS-XIX TO HAVE YOUR WORDS HEARD AS DEADLY

29DS-XX TO INCREASE UN-WELLNESS IN INCREMENTS

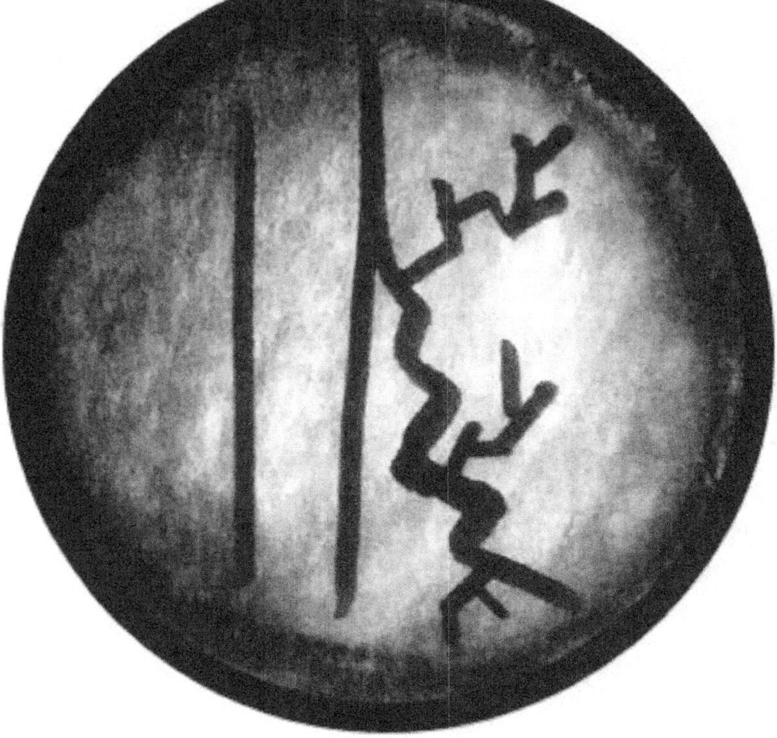

29DS-XXI TO ALLOW FOR PROFOUND AND OBVIOUS HUMILIATING DECLINING OF ANOTHER

29DS-XXII TO CAUSE ONE TO BE TRAPPED IN A LOOP

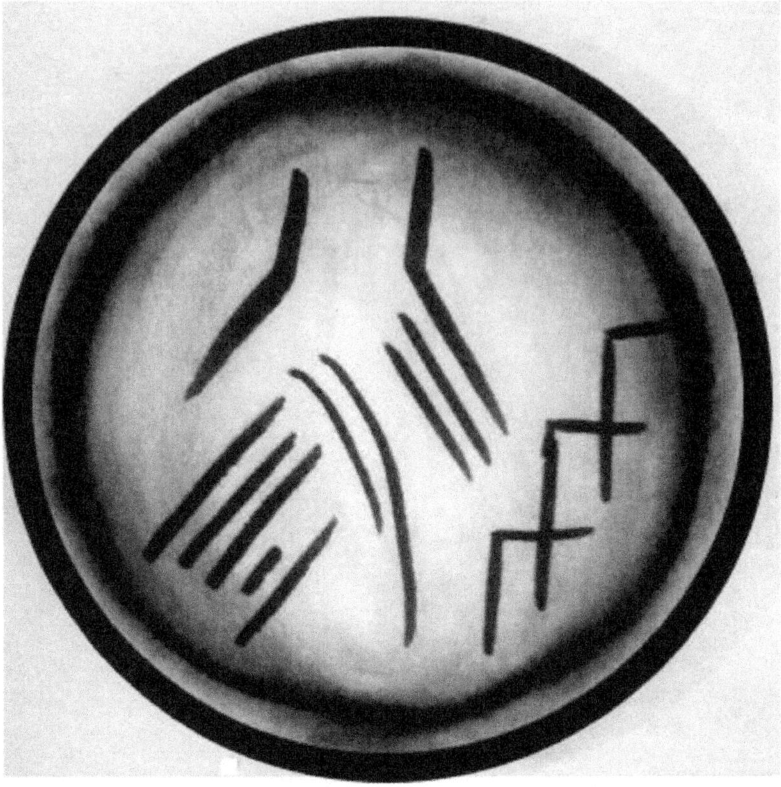

29DS-XXIII
TO FORCE SOMEONE TO LIVE IN THE PAST

29DS-XXIV TO MAKE SOMEONE VULNERABLE TO POSSESSION

29DS-XXV TO CAUSE ONE TO HEAR CONSTANT NOISE

29DS-XXV1 TO CAUSE A COMA THAT MIMICS DEATH

29DS-XXVII TO CAUSE A LANDLORD TO BE DESTROYED

29DS-XXVIII TO CAUSE A LIAR'S TONGUE TO SWELL AND CHOKE THEM

29DS-XXIX TO INVITE THE ACTION OF DEATH INTO SOMEONE'S HOME

BLANK PAGE FOR NOTES

NOTES ON TECHNIQUES

SPITTING, LICKING WITH YOUR TONGUE AND SWALLOWING OR INGESTING AS ACTS OF SORCERY

I bring to this work a vast history of experience and knowledge. During a long personal experience many years ago I was allowed entry into a certain North East museum's private library. There I studied original materials on "magic"…papyri and parchments, even several skins…

What came to me from this extravagant opportunity was not a single lightning bolt of clarity – but rather a moment of understanding that the human mind's interest in Sorcery (magic…if you prefer), is really formatted in one of two ways.

Theoretical magicians who approach the subject like an anthropological fascination, and the wild whip of a mind that knows that in real time one can change outcomes by some sort of adjustment of energy.

Some pepper this with boundaries of gods, deities and divinities – others with rules and regulations – and still others with boundaries of what they are and are not permitted to attain. Those of us who are completely unhinged from the ball and chain of those parameters see this as a profoundly important playground – one filled with all the opportunity a human mind can muster up – and then a thousand times more.

So we search...we experiment and we hustle through the modern day PC nonsense and we ultimately push through to the other side and realize we are in the dish with physics and opportunity and nothing more. We are in good company....

Humans therefore are the common thread through centuries of trying to make the rock turn to gold....and at the time of this writing I have no doubt that it has and will continue to...every one of us has a pet project....

I will be offering a book in the near future that addresses the following subject on a much broader scale, however for now I offer here what is necessary for the use of these sigils.

That being said, what I have noticed is that Sorcery has contained few “connectives” - things consistently present in ritual from the time humans walked upright tearing into animal flesh to appease some great force which threw water and fire from the sky upon their heads - to the present monotonous diatribe of those who write derivative books and encyclopedic works on these subjects with nothing new to offer….

The connectives are:

1. Blood
2. Saliva
3. Vengance

So I have written endlessly about Blood, and will, I am sure, continue to do so.

This book is based on the innate requirement for vengeance so there is no more to add on that subject as this book itself is the testament to the praxis (not a typo)of it.....

That leaves saliva....so here we go...

For the overall purpose of Sorcery – saliva has two categories of service.
Heal or Destroy...**Here we discuss the latter.**

One must turn the spittle in their mouths to poison and therefore the act of spitting it out is an accurate and focused poisoning of the Target.
For the purpose of this work, the work of sigils built to hard, gain control or destroy, one must develop a relationship between their own saliva and vengeance.

Daemons live in a sort of constant jealousy that powers their search for chaos. Inside of that on-going melee, their jealousy snakes a specific tangent towards the use of the actions of the human mouth.

They spend a great deal of time and effort observing the human mouth, which is precisely why it is so simple to ask them to crush liars.

Daemons lead a bivalent practice of egomaniacal self-gratification shifting between enjoyment of great hubris regarding their permeability, fluidity and ability to travel through time - and their lingering jealousy and desire to lean, sit, touch, fuck and spit.

This is how we develop relationships with Daemons, by allowing them access to these experiences through intentional temporary possession – however again I digress...

I will go on in this subject only to substantiate the importance of a relationship with one's saliva. Just as we have done in Blood Sorcery, take this opportunity to learn the flavors of your saliva – how it tastes when you are angry, happy, aroused, lost, exhausted or focused. Knowing this will allow for you to carefully place your oral biological into its best form the when need arises....

There are well over twenty words which can be used to denote the word "spittle" in the Egyptian language of the pharaonic period. Many of them link to words whose meanings are really rooted in washing or inundation. So prevalent was its usage that the hieroglyph of the spitting mouth evolved into the letter P in some of the later writings, especially those whose subject was Sorcery.

Of course, as proved in a multitude colloquialisms which have rolled all the way from Pharaonic Egypt (Book of the Dead, Spell 110 utilizes the verb construct "to spit", and then refers to the outcome as "conception") into current usage, there is an undeniable association to the Sorcery power of spittle being associated with semen as well.

So gentleman, feel free to make the exchange within the individual usages regarding the sigils.

I say gentleman because this particular set of twenty-nine sigils does not seem to take well to the use of exchanged or borrowed biologicals. THE BOY demands that all uses of biologicals are delivered from "their maker's body". Women who are utilizing these sigils will do just fine with their saliva, which is precisely why I suggested you get to know the mood of that particular fluid by taste.

As I mentioned in the Personal Foreword, when I feel anger my saliva immediately tastes like Blood. That has always been the case. When I was three, or seventeen or thirty eight or now, that has been a consistent expression. I took that experience into consideration when I realized that if that was happening consistently then there must be other changes in the taste of my saliva when I am in other moods. Linking success to success I was able to:

1. Learn the taste of my saliva when any one of a dozen moods were present
2. Consequently call **UPON** that specific taste when in requirement. An instant Elixir.....

The second one is what makes this viable Sorcery. In other words I can spit a biological that fits the requirement of the immediate Sorcery.

Consider this scenario. A person is bothering you in a bar. You have tried many courteous ways to assuage the individual to find you less interesting and to move along. What if you could speak into your finger with the purpose of the following action – then put that finger in your mouth and bring out the saliva required to make the perpetrator pass out, then dip it into the individual's drink? **Yes, that is doable, and that is Sorcery.**

EXERCISE

Do try the exercise previously listed as a scenario in a bar. Try it with the outcome being sleepiness, anxiety and generosity on the part of the Target.

I suggest this because utilizing your saliva will be a big part of the work with these sigils.

Look in the near future for a book I will offer on the expansion of the use of biologicals in these ways...

Now onto the sigils...

BLANK PAGE FOR NOTES

HOW TO USE THESE SIGILS
THREE OPTIONS

OPTION ONE – THE MOST EFFICIENT (more suited to – albeit not limited to students familiar with my work resulting in a honed on-going relationship with THE BOY through Effigy)

These sigils require an effigy and Blood. **Your Blood…** and in this, a perfect world of the usage of sigils provided by a Daemon, in this rare case your Blood will represent two worlds…others will tell you that this is not a good idea….that using your own Blood is somehow a "**no-no**" in the world of Sorcery. Those people are wrong…uninformed…and untrained…

First and foremost the sigil will represent YOU - and the powerful focus and commitment to the work...

Secondly the effigy of THE BOY will also allow the Blood to be seen as the Blood of the victim... For the first two options you will be required to make an effigy. There are two ways to do so. This effigy description is for this, the first option and is recommended for those who will be using these sigils repeatedly...

Create a permanent effigy of THE BOY. You can also get one on my site if this suits you.

www.cagliastrotheironring.com

Instructions for permanent effigy of THE BOY:

Use either clay (baked or air dried), or carve from wood, (whatever is more within your proclivity to do) in order to have a permanent "THE BOY". Either one must be honed with your Blood by placing newly harvested Blood directly from your skin onto the bottom of his feet and the back of his neck. **Then you are to spit saliva that has been thought about as an Elixir** in order to deliver a permanent association between yourself and this effigy. After this, you will be able to re-use the effigy.

This effigy must fit within the palm of your hand. His center must have an open area through which to place, and pass through the sigil.

All sigils must encounter water and then heat. This is mimicked by the moistening and then the scrolling of the sigil, so keep that in mind.

The center of the boy – the pass through area - must contain Iron. Either imbed an iron nail or create an Iron Ring with either a small iron ring or with iron filings. The image here has the circular opening encrusted with iron filings.

IRON
W
N
E
S

Prepare the sigils by either copying the one from the book (and you have permission to copy each sigil for the purpose of the ritual and only **at the time of its use**).

Do not stockpile copies as the action of creating each sigil is vital and must be done in its entirety at the time of each act of Sorcery.

You could also redraw them yourselves. NOTE – hand drawn sigils must have a similar density – it must come close to the amount of background density and shading that you see in the photo. (If you desire to have a copy sent to you, made by this author, please email…)

When your sigil is ready and available, you will harvest your Blood from just behind the second knuckle (closer to your palm) of your thumb and add it to the background of the sigil – in a sense becoming part of its landscape.

You should not trace over any of the elements in particular with your Blood – simply smear a drop of your Blood into the background of the sigil.

Language note – the "Target" is the person upon whom this work is directed.

THE BOY

THE BOY is a curious fellow. He enjoys two behavioral aspects that I have seen consistently. First, he enjoys the element of surprise, sneaking up behind his Target (or at very least hiding and peaking out as in the photo of him peeking out behind the railings). Secondly, he really likes to know exactly to whom he is talking. Therefore you should **write the name of the Target on the back of the sigil** (make sure the sigil is still facing in the right direction not upside down), and **include one or more** of the following:

1. a biological of the target smeared on or pinned to the sigil as applicable (hair is an option)
2. a small photo (pinned)

3. two comments, written in black ink, about the Target that sets them apart... This must include a description of a physical attribute (he has a mole, she has very long fingers and red hair etc..) and something that defines the preferences or tastes of the individual (he enjoys his coffee with 5 sugars, she likes opera)

4.

When you are done you will spit on the writing. I suggest you hone your saliva as previously discussed to bring about the biological product most suited to the action. Even if you are doing the sigil for yourself this is a required step.

When this is all set up, place a bit of warm water with a drop of your Blood and 5 drops of vodka or gin into a spray bottle (or atomizer if you are more suited to that type of device) and **lightly** spray-dampen the sigil on both sides. Also **lightly** spray the inside of the brazier. Empty out the bottle and always begin fresh with this process.

Roll up the sigil with sigil side outward, thereby containing the target information within the scroll. Place it through the front of his body so that it is balanced within the effigy of THE BOY.

IN THIS IMAGE the scroll is a circle with random images which I added so that the reader would not develop the idea that this was a directive for only one sigil. It is here only to show that the sigil drawing is facing outward unless otherwise indicated in individual instructions.

WHERE TO PUT THE EFFIGY

Altar is a word that allows for all cerebral manifestation of religious iconography, so I avoid it where I can. Religious zealots who do not respect the rights of others to participate in their own choices do not like that those of us who realize that the god-reliance is a bottomless pit. They cannot grasp that a human may have an apotropaic ability without reliance upon the floating genies. That being said – if one **allows** (ALLOW is a word with which my students are quite familiar) oneself to grasp that an altar is quite simply a place to put things that are separate and apart from the day to day table in one's home then the word is purposeful.

Choose a place not used to do homework, watch tv or eat a meal – a table – a surface of some sort meant only for your work of this nature… "sacred" in this sense means uninterrupted… Place a brazier on the altar as you will be burning the sigil.

Place THE BOY in such a place and for this purpose it must be a place that can be allowed to get quite dark so a room that is well lit all the time is not a good choice. You may also consider an outdoor altar if you feel it would be ignored by local beasts and would be sheltered in some way from the elements.

Place a magnet on the altar. Consider that the center-point of a compass. In this work we call that center-point a Human Compass and in many cases it is the "location" in some cases literally and in others virtually – of the Practitioner.

Make small markers of the polarities simply with black ink on paper. I prefer parchment or thick water color paper so the directional markers feel more like tiles.

N
W
E
S

Place them appropriately and accurately around the magnet. Over the center magnet place a small glass dish (stone or clay will work as well – no plastic please). It must balance on the magnet. Place the sigil half way through the center hole in THE BOY and place him in the direction you will see listed in each of the sigils. When the sigil has lasted there for 90 minutes check back to see if THE BOY has changed the direction in which he faces. If he has, turn him back to the prescribed direction and place a drop of your Blood on his body. This is the benefit of having a permanent THE BOY, as the longer you use him in this way the more he will do your bidding as he becomes honed with your Blood over multiple "workings". This is not the same as offering him your Blood without doing a working – THE BOY seeks revenge – it is through **THIS** act that he hones to you…

Wait another hour or so after the adjustment. If he has moved again – repeat the Blood anointment until he stops moving and check each 90 minutes. Once he has an understanding to stay firm in the standing toward the prescribed polarity then it is time.

Prepare a piece of coal for the brazier. Light it and ready it. Place another drop of your Blood on the burning coal and then take the sigil from THE BOY by removing it from his back. Place it on the hot coal just as it is – and allow it to burn. Once it is burnt then allow it all to cool down. Grind the remains in the brazier with a pestle.

Place remaining pins on the altar. Follow the individual sigil directive as to their disposal of the ashes.

OPTION TWO – FOR THOSE WHO ARE NEWER TO THE WORK

This is all done in the same way – the same procedure as the first option. HOWEVER – in this option the effigy of THE BOY is burnt as well. That is the one difference - that you **do not** wind up with a permanent effigy of THE BOY.

For those of you who decide to try this work without making a permanent connection to THE BOY, this is your preferred method.

First you can make an effigy by twisting brown paper into the form of a boy and securing it with cotton thread. No glue or artificial/plastic adhesives please....

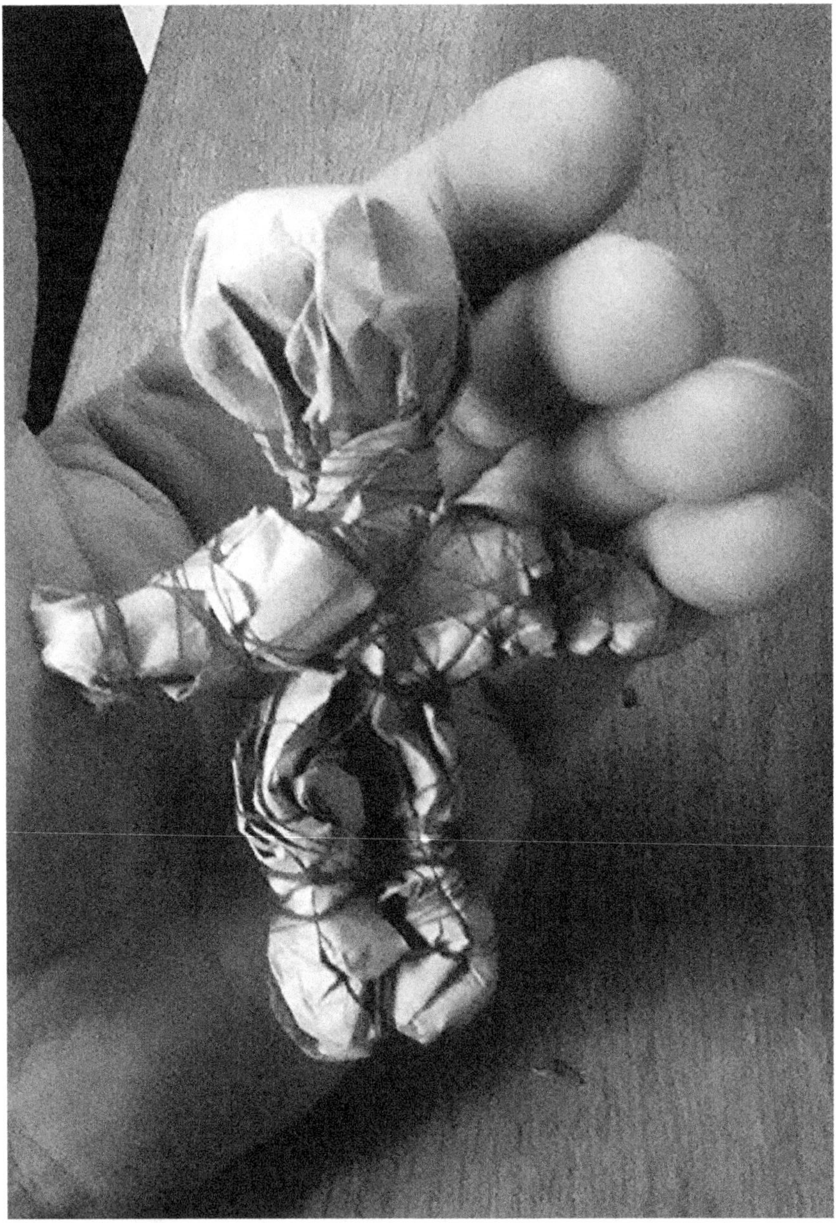

This effigy should also be small, and fit in the palm of your hand. The center should be hollowed out and iron must be added.

You will place an iron nail or iron filings on a natural adhesive such as honey or mud to hold the iron filings if you choose to use them.

N
S

The remainder of the instructions remain the same as the first option.

OPTION THREE - FOR THE SIMPLEST APPLICATION – THE "FUCK YOU CUPCAKE"

I had been using the term **"FUCK YOU CUPCAKE"** for the work of justice and revenge utilizing sigils…and it occurred to me that this had actual application.

Regarding the usage of the term, this book is the practical upgrade…
This is **"THE FUCK YOU AND PAY CUPCAKE"** book….get out your pans and little circular cupcake liner papers….

The previous two options have been very clear instructions for the usages of these sigils for those of you seeking advanced usage or a permanent relationship with THE BOY…

That being said some people just want to deliver one really nasty blow. Here is the shortcut which can be used by anyone – no matter what one's commitment is to the work or to the relationship to any particular Daemon.

Here goes…

For this shortcut version of the usage of these sigils (and the usage of other sigils in my work as well) – **lightly** redraw the sigil on baking parchment paper in pencil as accurately as you can. Then, also lightly in pencil, on the **back of the sigil** making sure the sigil is not upside down – write the following:

The name of the Target and two comments about the target that sets them apart… This must include (as in the general instructions) a description of a physical attribute (he has a mole, she has very long fingers and red hair etc…) and something that defines the preferences or tastes of the individual (he enjoys his coffee with 5 sugars, she likes opera)

Once again…when you are done you will spit on the writing. I suggest you hone your saliva as previously discussed to bring about the biological most suited to the action. Even if you are doing the sigil for yourself this is a required step.

Place a drop of batter into the cupcake liner, and then place the sigil in the bottom of a little cupcake liner **facing upwards** so that the sigil bakes into the batter.

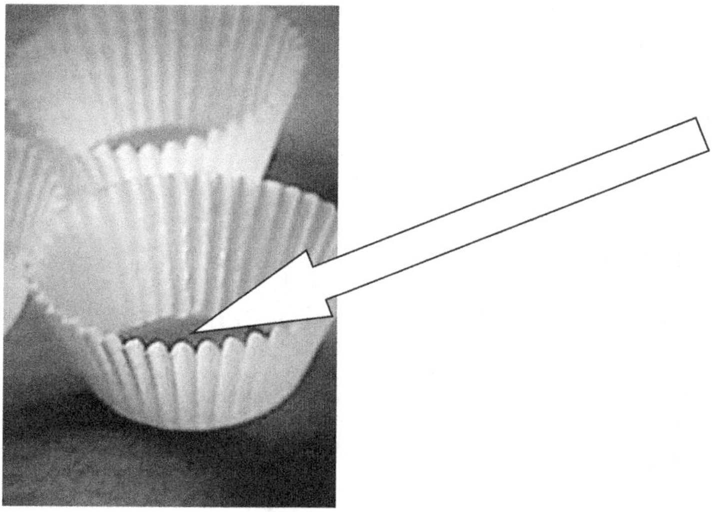

Now, – pour in the rest of the batter – bake and **serve to the Target**.....

ADDITIONAL NOTES ON THIS THIRD METHOD

Your results will depend on your commitment to this procedure as it lacks the polarity portion and the full complement of triggers we use in the Science of Sorcery. However to add an advanced application to this simple method, i.e., to best utilize the **"FUCK YOU CUPCAKE"** option, place the cupcake liner with the sigil inside in a Human Compass Set Up as listed in options One and Two for 90 minutes before filling it with batter. Then remove the sigil, add the first drop of batter, place the sigil back in, fill with batter, bake and serve to the Target…

BLANK PAGE FOR NOTES

SIGIL SPECIFICS

This section leaves the broad instructions and moves into the sigil-specific instructions. I have re-listed each sigil here with theirs specifics. Choose the one that best fits your requirements…

REMEMBER TO READ THROUGH ALL OF THE MATERIAL BEFORE BEGINNING ANY OF THESE PROCESSES.

This is good practice for all instructional materials regarding rituals and practices of this nature.

29DS-I TO ALLOW YOURSELF TO DO DAMAGING WORKS

This sigil is placed first because it is the most important one regarding honing the **self** – the Practitioner - to use these sigils and in general to use materials that produce these types of results.

I suggest everyone use this one first…

In this work, the shreds and remains of doctrine forced upon us when we were children still seep into our ability to protect ourselves.

I do a great deal of work with people who encounter the information that I offer regarding these types of matters and they contact me to say that they have been overwhelmed by the negative actions of others - yet they cannot bring themselves to pull the trigger on the use of sigils such as the powerful and focused ones herein. They are PC prisoners...

The use of this sigil will allow the user to move forward in the work. For this sigil – there is **one significant change** regarding the **"HOW TO"** use these sigils directive.

The practitioner will be putting their OWN information on the sigil....and then when it is all set up, place THE BOY on the dish resting on the magnet and place all four polarity markers on the dish with him.

N
S

Once the sigil has been transferred to the brazier and burning has been done, carry the remains in a leather pouch. Use the materials in the pouch on the rare occasion when a perpetrator is so difficult that the practitioner is concerned for their well-being. In those instances pin the image of the perpetrator to the back of one of the 28 remaining sigils (choose the best fit) and smear a tiny bit of the ash on the image of the perpetrator. Then work it in one of the two first options.

PLACEMENT OF THE ASHES – place in leather pouch as mentioned above

29DS-II
GO AHEAD....JUMP

POLARITY – NORTH EAST

Attaches to an already existing paranoia, self-doubt or sense of loss and speeds up the process.

PLACEMENT OF THE ASHES – throw them out of a window – a windy day is best. After tossing them, spit at them with a mindfulness of revenge. This will make sure that the Target knows you were the catalyst. If you do not desire the Target to know, then do not spit.

29DS-III
TO CAUSE SOMEONE TO LIE ALL THE TIME AGAINST THEIR WILL

POLARITY – NORTH WEST

Taps into their ability to tell the truth and speeds it up into a reflective situation causing the Target to say the opposite.

PLACEMENT OF THE ASHES – place them in beef and bury them in the driest soil you can find. Place your ring finger in your mouth and push the saliva into soil North West of the burial.

29DS-IV
TO STOP ANOTHER FROM FEELING JOY

POLARITY – SOUTH

Takes a sad or difficult moment and breaks all bonds between it and the possibility of repair or recovery.

PLACEMENT OF THE ASHES – bury on a child's grave and leave a toy as a tribute. Mimic (see in your mind) the name on the headstone to include the name of the Target.

29DS-V
TO CAUSE SOMEONE TO FOREVER DESIRE WHAT THEY CANNOT HAVE

POLARITY – WEST

Grabs the sensation of approaching attainment and misplaces the landing of the attainment while increasing the longing. In other words sending someone's joy elsewhere…

PLACEMENT OF THE ASHES – pour into an engine or some machine with moving parts and petrol. Don't speak, don't look back – walk away.

29DS-VI
TO TAKE AWAY SOMEONE'S ABILITY TO ORGASM

POLARITY – SOUTH

Breaks the bond between the target and sexual satisfaction

PLACEMENT OF THE ASHES – masturbate and rub your sexual fluids on a beef or bison bond. Mix the ashes into ground chicken meat. Place the bone and the chicken meat somewhere where birds can eat these materials.

29DS-VII
TO CAUSE ONE TO CONFESS TO A CRIME THEY DID NOT COMMIT

POLARITY – NORTH EAST

Puts an artificial requirement into the Target to solve the case by an admittance of guilt.

PLACEMENT OF THE ASHES – place near or on iron bars, or under a pile of nails or iron railroad spikes (railroad spikes are my personal first choice).

If that is not available place under a brick which is dusted with iron filing or covered in nails.

Make sure this is left in a public place. The more foot traffic the better. It doesn't matter if it is cleaned up or comes apart – as long as it is seen by others. Hone your saliva to enjoy the entertainment value of watching someone do this to themselves. Spit on the materials. Point to them and then walk away. Do something that you perceive to be self-indulgent.

29DS-VIII
TO KEEP ONE STUCK IN SORROW

POLARITY –EAST

Grabs hold of a sorrowful moment and perpetuates it into a habit for the Target.

PLACEMENT OF THE ASHES – Rub them on a mausoleum door where the door meets the ground or stone. Leave two flight feathers (long wing feathers) facing opposite directions.

Use two feathers from the same kind of bird.

Leave the feathers on the spot and make a commitment to be willing to listen if the Disincarnate buried within choose to speak to you. Do this in the daytime and wait there until after dark.

29DS-IX
TO INJECT ONESELF INTO SEXUAL DREAMS

POLARITY – NORTH EAST

Mimics a dream-state of the Target and places the Practitioner into the dream. Secondary step – **along with Blood – smear some sexual fluid obtained through orgasm on the FRONT of the sigil.**

PLACEMENT OF THE ASHES – Masturbate or enjoy a satisfying sexual encounter. When you are done, mix ashes with your fluids. Put some of the material into moving water that is pulling away from the spot on which you are standing. Place a small smear of the materials on a pillowcase what was in your bed during your sexual satisfaction, and keep the pillowcase in a dark drawer for as long as possible. This is a variation on the FLATLINE RITUAL (see BOOK CATALOG at the end of this book if you desire to do more forced dream work.)

29DS-X
TO STEAL AWAY THE LOVE OF AN "INFANT"

POLARITY – SOUTH WEST

Makes a child fall more in step and love with someone other than their parent. **This is a particularly brutal act. Choose carefully as the bond is permanent.** The Practitioner will have to choose the person who receives the child's love.

If it is to be the **Practitioner** who will receive that love – you must touch a lit wooden match to your skin - putting it out, and add the match to the inside of the sigil scroll. If the love is assigned to another person, then the image of **THAT** person must be **rolled around the sigil** scroll with the image facing **inward**.

PLACEMENT OF THE ASHES – bury them on the grave of a stillborn inside of a beautiful handkerchief, and give a gift anonymously to a living child. If you can find a living child who is **blind**, then that is the best choice as a recipient of the gift.

29DS-XI
TO SHUT SOMEONE'S MOUTH COMPLETELY

POLARITY –EAST

Each word spoken by the Target acts as an "engine" toward shutting the Target's mouth. This is a work of momentum which is supported by the East.

PLACEMENT OF THE ASHES –mix with molasses, fish Blood or smashed fish organs and poppy seeds and smear on a tar surface. Position yourself to spit on the mix, then don't - as you will not open your mouth.

29DS-XII
TO CAUSE DESTRUCTION THROUGH SUGGESTION OF POSSESSION

POLARITY – SOUTH WEST

Whisper the name of the Target into the scroll, alternating sides – many many times, then place it into THE BOY. Then keep a second copy of the image of the Target in a glass. Each day, over several days, pour red wine into the glass until the image is drowned.

During this time, if possible, ask the Target if they are ok as often as possible. At this point continue the method of the ritual.

PLACEMENT OF THE ASHES – give them to the Target. It is best if they know you have done Sorcery on them. If it is not possible to tell them, leave the ashes where they can see them.

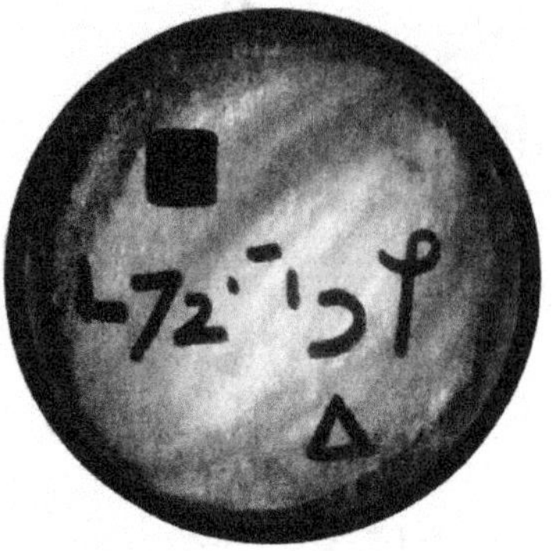

29DS-XIII
TO FORCE DISTANCE BETWEEN TWO HUMANS

POLARITY – SOUTH

Breaks the bond between two human beings.

PLACEMENT OF THE ASHES – draw two figures in hard dry underfed soil, and leave the ashes between them. Hone your saliva to think of flood waters. Spit on the feet of each of the two figures. Watch the soil absorb your saliva.

29DS-XIV
TO CAUSE SOMEONE TO FORGET THEIR IDENTITY

POLARITY – SOUTH

Separates someone **from themselves**. Very ugly business this....

PLACEMENT OF THE ASHES – divide them into two portions. Mail one half to yourself and don't open the envelope. Burn it again and combine the ashes with the remaining half of the original ashes.

Leave half of the mix strewn about in a public palace with high foot traffic and leave the remaining half in several old books in a library.

29DS-XV
TO CAUSE ONE TO SELF-DESTRUCT THROUGH GUILT

POLARITY – NORTH EAST

Spit on, then bury an image of the Target for three days and nights then dig it up and use it for the sigil work. Make sure the soil has stained it.

PLACEMENT OF THE ASHES – Leave it on the Target's property or amongst her/his belongings. If you can put it in their shoes then it is a perfect situation…

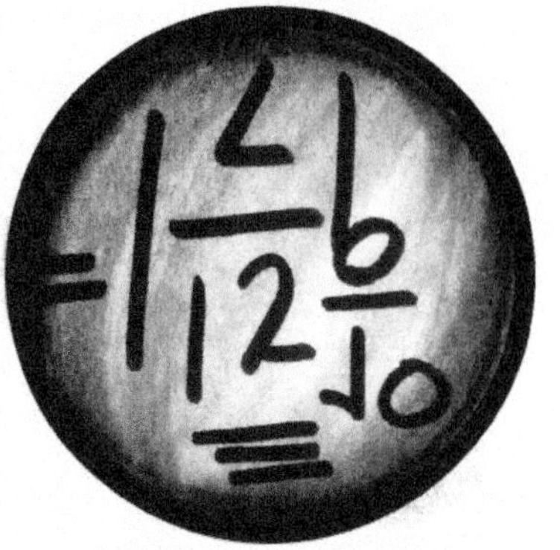

29DS-XVI
TO ENCOURAGE SELF-LOATHING

POLARITY – SOUTH
Breaks the bonds with self-acceptance

PLACEMENT OF THE ASHES – Best case scenario is that you can get the Target to eat or smoke them. If not place them somewhere where they will be in the Target's breathable air. If the Target is a lover then put a bit on your lips and kiss them. We are looking for ingestion by the Target here.

29DS-XVII
TO CAUSE SOMEONE TO THINK THEY ARE SOMEONE ELSE OF YOUR CHOICE

POLARITY –EAST

A seed of another personality is planted and is set upon to grow rapidly

PLACEMENT OF THE ASHES –Leave the ashes with the person you chose the Target to believe they are. Put them inside of a plant or gift – make a choice that gives the presence of the ashes with the other person longevity and causes them to be "seen" regularly. When that is done and the ashes are firmly set into the other person's life/home, take any belonging from that person and give it to the Target.

29DS-XVIII

TO MAKE SOMEONE PAY, WITH THEIR WELLNESS OR LONGEVITY, FOR WASTING YOUR TIME OR TRUST (THE BROTHER SIGIL TO THE POISONER'S SIGIL)

POLARITY – NORTH EAST

Brings the lost time into the Sorcery arena and opens a tab…

PLACEMENT OF THE ASHES – Rub a bit of the ashes on money and find a way for the Target to get that money. Mix the remainder of the ashes in with coins and bury on your property on keep secluded in your home.

29DS-XIX
TO HAVE YOUR WORDS HEARD AS DEADLY

POLARITY – WEST

The west carries sound. In this case you are placing your comments into the West to utilize and exploit this mechanism. As this is one of the few sigils in this group that has application to be used on and by the practitioner, if used on the self then use the match technique here as well.

Technique for the self - Light a wooden match and put it out on your skin. Place it inside of the scroll.

For use on someone else who has this desire for their own words to be received this way, place a photo of them around the outside of the sigil with the photo side facing OUTWARD.

In both cases if there is a particular person **to** whom the words must sound deadly – place that individuals materials on the back of the sigil.

If the request is a general one – to make ones words sound deadly in general – make 2 copies of the sigil, smear your Blood on both of them, place them back to back and proceed with all of the other parts of the process listed in the **"HOW TO"** section.

PLACEMENT OF THE ASHES – Mix into wax and make a candle – give it to someone you feel is strong and powerful. Take something of theirs and cut it in two. If you did this sigil on your own behalf keep both pieces. If you did the sigil on someone else's behalf give one half to that person and keep the other.

29DS-XX
TO INCREASE UN-WELLNESS IN INCREMENTS

POLARITY – SOUTH
Breaks bonds with healing.

PLACEMENT OF THE ASHES – Place on a well trafficked road bed. Spit resentment onto them. Watch for the first car to run them over. Look away from the ashes.

29DS-XXI
TO ALLOW FOR PROFOUND AND OBVIOUS HUMILIATING DECLINING OF ANOTHER

POLARITY – SOUTH

Breaks bonds with the normal "ladder" /process human beings experience when trying to regain footing in a bad situation.

PLACEMENT OF THE ASHES –

Sharpen a pencil into the ashes until the pencil cannot be further sharpened.

Place the mixture back on a burning coal with a fresh berry. Burn until the wood shavings are ashes and the berry is decrepit. Put half in an unmarked envelope and mail to the Target. Bury the other half in the grave of a single woman under thirty years of age. Leave your Blood on the headstone as a tribute.

29DS-XXII
TO CAUSE ONE TO BE TRAPPED IN A LOOP

POLARITY – WEST

Just as it feels like the Target is coming out of it – the loop begins over again…

PLACEMENT OF THE ASHES – Put the ashes in a circle of cloth along with a second copy of the sigil. Lick both sides of the sigil. Hang high in a tree so that you can see them. Leave there until it rots away.

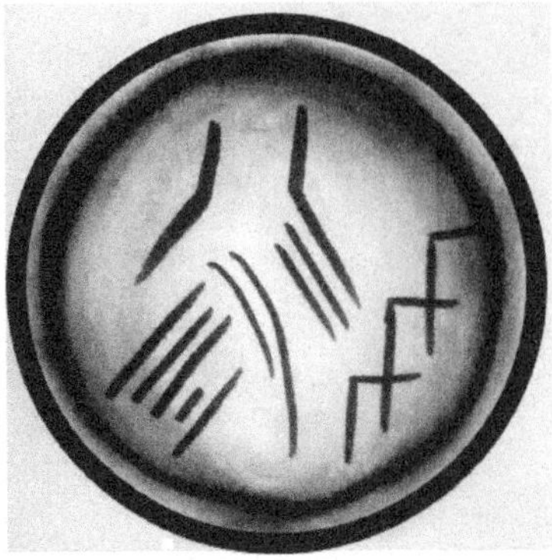

29DS-XXIII
TO FORCE SOMEONE TO LIVE IN THE PAST

POLARITY – SOUTH EAST

This effects the ability for someone to move forward and to become melancholy regarding the past.

PLACEMENT OF THE ASHES – This is a trigger usage. Find a dead animal whose death had nothing to do with you. Roadkill is perfect for this so go take a drive on a rural roadway. Pick up the animal and put it in a box.

Drive it back to a direction from which it most likely came. This is simple to figure out by which way its Blood has dragged or spattered. This will work only when that direction is correct. If this does not yield results do again until this is accurate. Place the animal on soil facing the direction in which it was **FOUND**. Then roll the ashes in a circle of cotton fabric and put the ashes into either the animal's mouth – or cut open the belly an place the ashes inside. Then turn the animal back to the direction FROM WHICH it came, and walk away.

29DS-XXIV
TO MAKE SOMEONE VULNERABLE TO POSSESSION

POLARITY – NORTH

Increases a person's "charisma" to Daemons, and opens up a portal to possession.

Advanced Practitioners can utilize one of the Daemons in 26 Daemons Revisited here to be specific (see BOOK CATALOG at the end of this book)

DO NOT USE PITCHER JOHN.
Place that Daemon's sigil facing against the back of the sigil from this book so that it covers the information you have written about the Target.

PLACEMENT OF THE ASHES – they must blow away toward the North – if there is no wind, "intent" for some....

29DS-XXV
TO CAUSE ONE TO HEAR CONSTANT NOISE

POLARITY – EAST

This picks up on a repetitive noise that upsets or antagonizes the Target and puts it in a loop in the Target's ear,

PLACEMENT OF THE ASHES – pour them onto railroad tracks (THE BOY's idea) or inside a computer tower (my idea).

29DS-XXV1

TO CAUSE A COMA THAT MIMICS DEATH

POLARITY – SOUTH

Breaks the bond with life and liveliness. Mimics a coma onto the Target. **Coma** may mean that the person loses all ability to function and move forward.

The Target may begin to decline slowly and then decay into an actual immobility.

PLACEMENT OF THE ASHES – Place some of them into the Target's liquid soap or shampoo or water source. Continue to do so over a bit of time until they are gone.

If you do not have access then make an effigy of the person using a commercial doll that can get wet. Buy liquid soap to use ONLY FOR THE EFFIGY OF THE TARGET. Add the ashes. "Shower" the effigy nightly until you have used all of the soap. Bury the soap container and the effigy in wet sand.

29DS-XXVII
TO CAUSE A LANDLORD TO BE DESTROYED

POLARITY – NORTH

Picks up on the hubris of the landowner at hand (the Target) and puts them in dangerous situations which are honed to push the tipping point. This presents dangerous situations thereby causing others to become violent ultimately causing the immobility and/or demise of the landlord.

PLACEMENT OF THE ASHES – Simple – sprinkle them on her property or living space (not in your living space)….smear them on the rent check, use sparingly until all gone….she will be all gone as well…

29DS-XXVIII
TO CAUSE A LIAR'S TONGUE TO SWELL AND CHOKE THEM

POLARITY – EAST

Causes suppression of air, an increase in Blood flow **into** the area causing compression and a decrease of Blood flow OUT of the area.

Roll up a few yards of black thread, lick it until it is damp and place it inside of the sigil scroll.

PLACEMENT OF THE ASHES – put them in beef or pig fat. Burn until only blackness is left. Divide the burnt remains and place half on the property or living space of the liar and bring half to a swamp or somewhere dirty and wet. Spit "venom" on them, drop them there and walk away.

29DS-XXIX
TO INVITE THE ACTION OF DEATH INTO SOMEONE'S HOME

POLARITY – NORTH WEST

Allows the action and identity of Death in. If there are animals in the house and you don't desire to hurt them (which is suggested as they are vulnerable) place the fur or feather of a domestic animal **inside** the sigil before you roll it.

Then make a notch in the circle around the sigil (scales from fish and lizards will not work). That will separate the animals from the Death experience.

PLACEMENT OF THE ASHES – A swamp or marshland is required. If you do not have one nearby then you will have to create a filthy little wet "pond". For 31 nights you will bring a bit of the ash to such a place. Each night you will harvest your Blood – touch it only with your mouth by sucking it from the wound – throw in the ashes and spit the Blood. On the last night decapitate a fish and throw the head West and the body North.

Be very sure about this before you proceed....

BLANK FOR NOTES

CLOSING COMMENTS

This book is brutal, these sigils are brutal, THE BOY is brutal and I am brutal when intentionally crossed. Let this be a clear warning to those who mistake kindness for weakness.

THE BOY is a Daemon, and a Daemon without a conscience. He doesn't care if you destroy your stalker, cause eternal pain for someone who stole from you, put someone into an unforgiving loop of sorrow when they posed as a friend and became a poacher of ideas and favors….and neither do I.

This is not a PC tome. I have a list of individuals, just as you do, who have crossed the line of trust with intent and malice – go ahead – admit it to yourself. You may have better access to that list after you use the first Sigil, 29DS – I.

I don't care if your world is polluted with fools who use you like a paper towel and toss you away – however YOU SHOULD CONSIDER CARING about that.

I'm just a dealer – making the weapons of visceral and devastating sigils and the Daemons that bring them available on your doorstep. There they are – rolled up on your welcome mat like your daily paper. Hey – it is up to you to put on your slippers and go round them up…

I am in possession of a grade A mind, an endless number of Disincarnate with which to communicate, and a powerful structure of Attending Daemons so committed to my well-being that they have no time to participate in nonsense. I am much like them as neither do I...

To those who have studied, and continue to study with me, my wonderful and brilliant students, and to the members of THE FIRM, to my loved ones and real friends, and to Toy and the Master Student who make advancement possible, I say the following...you will for-ever have my protection....

To those of you who feel you can drop in – use me or assume you know me – stop by, THE BOY and I are making tea....

SORCERESS CAGLIASTRO

BIO AND BOOK CATALOG

THE SORCERESS CAGLIASTRO
THE SORCERESS CAGLIASTRO
Author, Publisher, Teacher, Designer… Creator of the Science of Sorcery, the foremost authority on Blood Sorcery and Necromancy in the hands of 9……and creator of THE FIRM….. an elite hidden group of Sorcerers working together to produce broad stroke results…

This book is published by Iron Ring Publishing. The Sorceress owns another publishing company which prints original works of all kinds from other writers as well as the esteemed series RESCUED KNOWLEDGE PROJECT…for Publishing info on North Sea Tales visit **www.northseatales.com**

For more information about The Science of Sorcery or to study with The Sorceress Cagliastro visit **www.cagliastrotheironring.com** or Email sorceresscagliastro@gmail.com

TITLES FROM BOTH OF THE FOLLOWING LISTS CAN BE FOUND AT

amazon.com/author/sorceresscagliastro

TITLES BY IRON RING PUBLISHING

The Science of Sorcery Beginner Course Vol 1 (NECESSARY FOR BEGINNERS)

Blood Sorcery Bible Vol 2 – Striking the Target the Practitioner and the Static Practice (BEST IN THE SERIES)

Blood Sorcery Bible Vol 1 – Rituals in Necromancy

Blood Sorcery Bible Vol 1 Workbook

DIVINATION

23 Sigils of Selfish Indulgence

25 Sigils, Dark Circles from the Iron Ring

26 Daemons Revisited

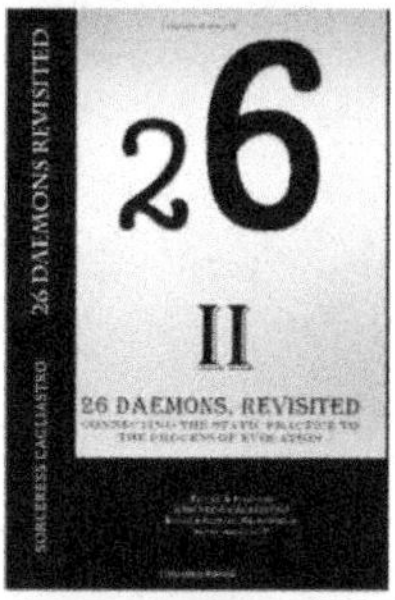

26 Daemons Workbook

Flatline Ritual, vengeance through dream interruption

Menstrual Blood and Semen – A Sorcery Manual

Al Vostro Servizio

Al Vostro Servizio Due

TITLES BY NORTH SEA TALES PUBLISHING

LEONA RETURNED – Script

Mini stories of justice: 7 really scary tales and lots of undeserved consequences

"…and then Minami's baby died…" ORIGINAL BOOK

"...and then Minami's baby died..." SCRIPT

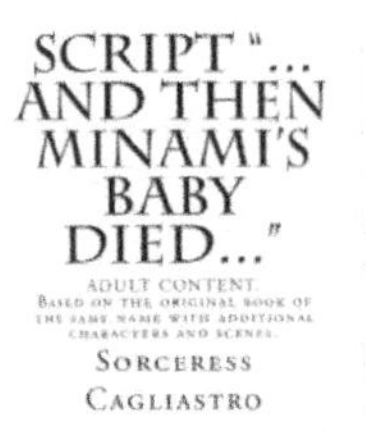

RESCUED KNOWLEDGE PROJECT published by <u>North Sea Tales</u>:

+CREE AND ENGLISH, a primer, originally published 1890

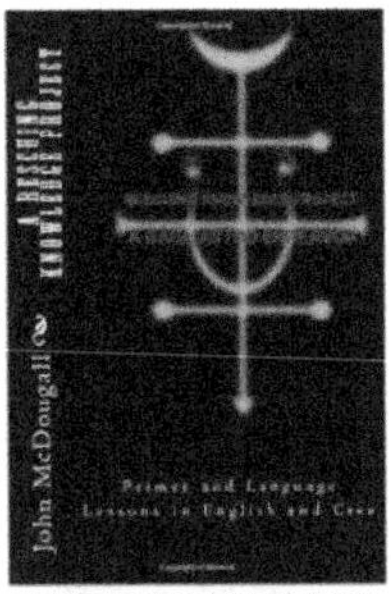

WORLDS FAIR COOK BOOK , originally published 1893

DEALINGS WITH THE DEAD, originally published first in 1856

MONEY MAKINGFORMULAS from the National Scientific Laboratories published first in1921

+DEVISES AND EMBLEMS originally published in 1699

ICE BREAKERS originally published 1819

UPCOMING NOVEL
Collette Mandolino Begins to Cry
expected by April 2016

THE BOY effigy in clay is available at **www.cagliastrotheironring.com**

CONTACT INFORMATION

For author information or for submission guidelines for North Sea Tales please visit www.northseatales.com or contact **northseatales440@gmail.com**

For your Sorcery Requirements, Readings/Consultations, to become a student of the Science of Sorcery, or for information about THE FIRM sorceresscagliastro@gmail.com

BLANK PAGE FOR NOTES

BLANK PAGE FOR NOTES

BLANK PAGE FOR NOTES

Made in the USA
Middletown, DE
09 April 2025

74018976R00096